LIVIN(

by
Fr Andrea Gasparino

All booklets are published thanks to the
generous support of the members of the
Catholic Truth Society

CATHOLIC TRUTH SOCIETY
PUBLISHERS TO THE HOLY SEE

2

CONTENTS

HOLY COMMUNION:
GRAFTING US INTO THE DIVINE LIFE

Holy Communion should be the point within the Mass which finds us most attentive, it is the moment of a personal meeting with Jesus himself.

At every other time in the Eucharistic liturgy we interact with the sacrament together with our brothers and sisters, as part of the Christian community, and our responsibility is shared with them.

The moment when we take Communion is somehow different. It is the awesome moment in which we have a face to face meeting with Jesus Christ. He meets with us personally and has a dialogue with us. He comes to choose us because he has something special to say to us, something which is for our ears only. It is a moment in which we come before Christ alone.

In the liturgy of the Word we hear the readings together with all our brothers and sisters around us. A priest proclaims the Gospel to us and everything is ordered to ensure we listen well. However in Communion we have a one to one with Christ and we come before him in all our weakness, with all our sins and our unworthiness.

A dramatic and privileged moment

Holy Communion is a moment of high drama and privilege. Woe to us if we do not realize this. If we come to the meeting with Christ unprepared we risk ruining the encounter altogether, and the responsibility lies with us alone.

There is always the risk that we take Communion without thinking sufficiently about it. We don't disrespect the Eucharist on purpose but often it is simply a case of being distracted. When this happens it is always a missed opportunity and damages our friendship with Christ.

It is vital that we realize the full extent of our responsibility. When Jesus meets people in the gospels their life is invariably changed forever. In the gospel there are many examples of these crucial meetings: Zacchaeus, the adulterous woman, Levi, the Samaritan woman, Peter, Andrew and James... How many times have we met with Christ in Holy Communion and what has changed? Nothing?

This could be the tragic reality in which we find ourselves. One worthy Communion is enough to make of us a saint, and yet all these Communions we have made have perhaps not moved us one inch from mediocrity.

From one Eucharist to another

The seriousness of the problem would hit home if we had the patience to sit down, take some paper and a pen and do some arithmetic. Think of how many times we take Communion in a year and then subtract the number of Communions that effected a change in our lives.

The crux of the problem lies exactly in this: what difference has the unique privilege of a personal meeting with Christ made to my life?

It is easy for us to be ungrateful, superficial, even blasé. We float along with indifference, drifting from one Eucharist to the next. Would it not be a good time to stop and think?

The reflections in this booklet have been written exactly for this, to help us to stop and think...

THE FIRST STEP

We need to make many changes to bring order to our Communions. It may not be possible to change everything that needs changing, since that would mean starting with the distant past, beginning with the preparation we received for our first Communion. Let us begin with more immediate concerns. The first step is to know whether or not we can receive Communion at Mass.

Once upon a time the problem was getting people to make more frequent Communions; nowadays there is the opposite problem. How does one stop people from taking Communion or at least give them a notion of the seriousness of what they are doing?

This problem was confronted with great severity by St Paul when he wrote to the Christian communities in Corinth (*1 Cor* 11:27).

Before Communion it is important to ask oneself a question: does my conscience permit me to receive Communion?

It is of no consequence that everyone else goes up for Communion. We must answer to our own conscience as to whether we can or can't, whether we are in friendship with Christ or whether we have broken off that friendship. Our conscience is not our imagination; our conscience should be the echo of the mind of the Church, the judgement of the Church.

If we are in a state of grave sin this would normally mean that before going to receive Communion we would need to go to confession and to do so in a state of sincere repentance. If a serious sin is connected to an ongoing situation then we must be even more careful, otherwise we can further aggravate our responsibility.

For this reason it is important to have a frank and reasoned conversation with a priest who in all honesty can state his understanding of the Church's judgement on our particular situation. In order to receive Communion it may be necessary to think long and hard, to confess and to change our behaviour.

If therefore, a conscience that is formed according to the mind of the Church, and not our religious ignorance, tells us that we should not receive Communion in that liturgy, then we should desist. We should remain in thoughtful silence before the Lord and in all humility ask for his help to come out of our particular situation.

If however, we are unsure as to whether our situation is serious enough to impede us from receiving Communion, if we feel that our particular circumstances may not add up to a serious sin, but still we are not sure, what should we do? Normally in these cases we should go and receive Communion, because in cases where there is doubt, the law is not binding. In this case it is important that the following signs of good will can be found in us: sorrow for our faults and weaknesses, a strong desire to cut with evil and a firm intention to come out of our situation of sin and the resolve to make the effort needed.

In matters of conscience, certainty is not always possible. Therefore in situations where there is some doubt and the three conditions mentioned above are met, one should go to Communion. Nevertheless, we should not isolate our doubt, and leave it unresolved. In gratitude for the gift that Christ gives us we should make an effort to confront the problem with clarity. As soon as the chance arises, go to speak with a priest and tell him the problem.

Make of your Communion a moment to meet with Christ and ask for light and strength. Light to understand and strength to win. Christ is close to all who struggle, and those who struggle do so for love. Who struggles against his sin is in friendship with Christ and Christ will help him in his struggle.

INTERRUPTING THE ROUTINE

We have already mentioned that as Christians we are grafted into the divine life, and began by saying that the main moment in which this takes place is the Eucharist.

I want to make it clear however, that the there are two moments of Communion in the Mass, although often they are not recognised as such. The first Communion is with the Word of God, and the second is with the Body and Blood of Christ. The two are interdependent.

Every time we go to Mass we should remember that we go and make two Communions. If we do, the Mass will have more meaning for us. First we should communicate with the Word, and we can do this no matter what situation we find ourselves in. Then if our conscience allows, we can make the second Communion with the Body and Blood of Christ.

I will speak at some length of the second Communion but what I say regarding it can also be applied to the Communion with the Word.

I will speak of the latter because it is often here that our Christian life falls into the tragic trap of being just another routine action.

Cold Communions

For those who take Communion often, it is easy to see that our personal meeting with Christ can soon say very little to us. It is sad but true that all of us have a predisposition for making Communion a banal event: an empty ritual where we are absent and it seems that Christ also is absent, where we become easily distracted and it seems that Christ also fails to speak. And as with every mode of behaviour, this shameful state of affairs can become a habit. These cold Communions can become so common that we stop even feeling bad about them.

So begins the tragedy of the cold Eucharist which doesn't help straighten anything in our life. Thus, our life in Christ is ruined at its root since it is not well nourished by the Eucharist.

We must succeed in breaking out of our routine, at any cost. But how? Perhaps we should find a system or technique to break out of our routine.

It should be simple, suitable for all and adaptable to all, and mindful of the liturgical aspects of Holy Communion.

Perhaps one solution could be to make an analogy with the visit of an old friend. In that situation what do we do?

When a friend comes home

When a much loved friend comes to visit, the first thing we do is to make a fuss over him, to celebrate his arrival.

We then hurry to offer him something to eat or drink. If we know him very well we will already know what he likes best and will not delay to offer him exactly that.

It doesn't even cross our mind to ask him to do something for us, rather we decide on the most suitable place in the house to sit and talk. We speak with him of the things we know interest him or allow him to speak as much as possible.

If then, there is something that we need to ask him to do for us, we know that he will want to help. Especially if the problem is a delicate or difficult one. We ask him at the end almost as a parting request.

This could well be a good model of behaviour when we think of how best to live Holy Communion. If we succeed in doing this, we will come out of our routine for sure, and Communion will again become a life-giving encounter.

1. Begin by celebrating. Impose it on yourself, as an act of faith. Express all your joy to Christ because you are meeting with him again. There is no need to speak or to have great thoughts or visions. For us to be happy in his presence is the most logical thing in the world, and it is equally logical to learn to express that happiness.

2. Offer something. But what? Something that will please God! Try to come to Holy Communion with a gift already ready: an act of charity (something done in order not to meet with Christ with empty hands), and straight after Communion, offer a future act to Christ. Bring an act of charity you have already done and promise a new one to Christ; it will help to link the Eucharist to your daily life, to our duty as Christians, to our acts of charity.

Offer something important to Christ, something that costs a lot, a courageous gift, some service given to a poor or old or sick person. A charitable action carried out within your own home is especially valuable.

3. Most importantly, listen! It is in listening that Christ waits to meet us. If Jesus instituted this special way of meeting with us, it was not by accident. He has something important to say to us. We should give Christ an opportunity to speak with us, or at the very least not put obstacles in the way of his words. If we are absent then we will not hear anything. He comes for a personal meeting with us.

If we receive Communion absent-mindedly then by definition we are not completely present. How can Christ touch us if we are not there.

So, we must make every effort to listen. Listening happens only when we truly want to communicate with God. He is always speaking to us but we fail to pick up the receiver, and he waits, because he never infringes our freedom.

It is precisely on this point that we can test the vitality of the Communion we have made. After every Communion we should be able to say exactly what God told us. Going home after Communion we should be able to say: "God said this to me".

We must, however, take care that our communication with God is not imaginary, that it does not take place in our imagination. Christ really does speak to us. We need to find out how, and we will look at this in detail later in this booklet. Christ does not need much to give us a word of life. He doesn't need many words nor great leaps of imagination. Christ can even speak to us through silence.

We need to persevere on this point, and firmly expect to communicate with Christ and to know after each Communion what he expects of us.

4. Then ask. He awaits our petitions. We must discover the power of the prayer that says: "Lord, if you want, you can heal me!" This was the prayer of the sick, the blind, the paralytics and the lepers. We should ask as the disciples did, to learn how to pray: "Master, teach us how to pray!" We must ask for the gift of light: "Speak Lord, your servant is listening"; "you have the message of eternal life". Above all, we must ask to do his will: "Lord, not mine but your will be done."

Now, imagine if you will, how your week would go if your Communion on Sunday were done properly, if the routine we slip into were broken. Imagine a whole month of proper Communions, each one a true personal meeting with Christ.

If we but think that it was enough to meet Christ once for a person's life to be completely changed, and then remember the hundreds, even thousands of times we have met Christ in the Eucharist and failed to communicate with him! How many miracles have passed us by?

How many times did we make it impossible for Jesus to act? He touched us and we didn't respond. He came to us but we did not communicate with him, and we failed to attain the fruits of our meeting with him.

In the following pages we will examine point by point the moments in which we can meet Christ, in order to see how we can correct our routine way of doing things. Let us begin with listening.

LISTENING: DIFFICULT BUT VITAL

Luke the Evangelist tells the story of Zacchaeus meeting Jesus and gives us a perfect blueprint to follow in learning to make our own Communion. In that meeting four actions occur that can be for us a model of thanksgiving.

1. There is a celebration: Zacchaeus "welcomed Him with joy."

2. There is an offering: Zacchaeus gives Jesus hospitality in his own home, and he surely treated Jesus to a fine feast too, as was the custom for a guest of honour.

3. Zacchaeus listened: and having listened, his response was impressive: "Zacchaeus got up and said 'Look, sir, I am going to give half my property to the poor, and if I have cheated anybody I will pay him back four times the amount."

4. He made a request: In all his actions there was an implicit desire to be saved: "today salvation has come to this house."

Listening is vital

Of the four actions listed above, listening is the most important. It is from listening that our personal response to Christ begins, the response that Christ asks of us.

Our response to the Eucharist is of vital importance, Christ does not come for nothing. He instituted this unique privilege for us so as to elicit a response, and the response is dependent on having heard the request.

The action of listening puts our friendship with Christ to the test, and we risk all when we take the Eucharist unthinkingly. It is like a friend who comes to visit us and spend a few hours with us. He knows we are in but we don't bother to open the door. Our discourteous response could put our whole friendship at risk.

To a friend such behaviour is truly offensive. And yet this is often how we welcome Christ in Holy Communion. He comes to search us out and we do not want to be found, many times simply because our heads are filled with thoughts other than the contemplation of the presence of Christ. Our cold welcome for Christ must be truly saddening to him, and what is worse is that we are so used to doing it. Listening during Communion is the most urgent and obvious action we should do during Communion, yet it is the one thing we forget most often. If you meet a friend and speak with him, then minutes later can't remember what you spoke about, you might as

well not have met at all. How many times does it happen
that after our meeting with Christ we cannot remember
what he said?

Listening is difficult

Listening is an activity which is at the same time active
and passive. As humans we tend to deal better with active
tasks than with passive ones. Talking is an active task,
being in silence is a passive one; but true listening means
being in silence and then acting. In listening there is give
and take, passivity and activity together.

Listening to God is difficult, for he is beyond our
bodily senses. We can stay for hours conversing with
somebody sitting in front of us, who responds and reacts
and asks questions. But we find it difficult to stay with
someone who says nothing. If we can't even see that
other person who says nothing, for example he or she is
on the other end of a telephone line, then we would find it
even more difficult.

In Holy Communion we are in a still more difficult
position. He is present, real and alive, in front of us, but
we perceive nothing. If we could at least hear him... If he
said one word to us that we could hear, yet this never
seems to happen. Therefore listening becomes
increasingly difficult, for even if we enter into dialogue
with God, it soon seems to become a monologue... and
what's more, a monologue delivered to an absent listener.

Yet we do need to meet with Christ, because it is he who comes to dwell in us, and we need to be there to receive him, and not be absent.

Since listening during Communion is so difficult it is the part that is most often left to one side. Speaking, reading, meditating, even whispering a prayer, all of these are easier than really listening. And yet the critical act at Communion is that of listening. If we take Communion and make no response then it is hardly a communication. He has done his part but we have failed in ours.

How to listen

In order to listen to Christ in Holy Communion we need some equipment. If we have it then Christ can speak to us; if we don't, he cannot.

The atmosphere around us is full of radio waves but we hear nothing with the naked ear. Yet, with a small transistor radio we can begin to tune in to the frequencies around us. In the same way, to be able to tune in to God's voice we need a particular transistor made up of three things: silence, the desire to communicate with God and the beginnings of a love for him.

Silence

God tends not to speak in the midst of a racket. We are not referring to external noise, which is the least of our problems. We are speaking of interior noise, the disorder, vanity and worldliness in which we live our lives.

Silence is for us a time of expectancy, of openness. Internal silence does not come naturally, we need to work at it. It normally requires space. It is impossible for us to say, out of the blue, "I will now be silent" because it is not enough to say it; sometimes it is not even enough to want it. We need to earnestly desire it from the bottom of our heart.

Such deep desires do not come easily. A long time is needed to get to the depths that exist within us, to penetrate the many levels of superficiality that envelop our lives. This silence exists in the lower reaches of our inmost selves.

Interior silence also requires a certain purification and detachment from ourselves.

It is not easy but it is possible for every person of good will to achieve the silence they need.

The desire to communicate with God

God respects our freedom, and if we want to cut ourselves off from him he will rarely go against our wish.

To those who have a true desire to communicate with God, those who wish to hear his voice, who want to discern his will, he will invariably answer. He does however, often keep us waiting a little while. Not on a whim but in order to prepare us.

Without the effort of waiting and listening we might not even catch his voice, which is imperceptible to our senses and barely audible to our soul. It takes only a little to suffocate God's voice within us. But he does speak, and what things he says! He speaks not to the ears but directly to the heart.

The beginnings of a love for him

Within us there must be a true desire to respond to him, to give him what he asks for, to accomplish what he wants of us, so that there may always be within us the first beginnings of a response: "speak Lord your servant is listening".

Practical ways of listening

When we are in the right frame of mind to listen, we then need to have the right equipment to listen to God. How can we facilitate a dialogue with him?

One very easy way is to slowly repeat to ourselves a word of God that particularly struck us during that liturgy. God speaks through the scriptures, it is, so to speak, his primary means of communication.

There is nothing better than listening attentively during the Liturgy of the Word, to see what God has to say specifically to us that day. There is always something if we listen carefully. There is much to gain if during

Communion we repeat that word to ourselves calmly and carefully. We can give God the time to engage with us.

Through a word of scripture listened to and welcomed with faith, God manifests himself: he speaks, he bursts forth into our lives.

Another practical way of listening to God in Communion is this: to reflect on the principal duties of that day and ask God what he expects of us in each of them.

Often in examining our principal duties, we will hear the voice of God speaking to our Spirit, urging us, helping us to reflect, to desire to do better, guiding our decisions, sometimes leading us to repentance.

Another way is to think of the principal problems that face us, those which worry us most.

We can run the risk of making of our problems greater than the person of Christ with whom we are trying to communicate, but sometimes it is necessary to call our problems to mind, saying to Christ: "Lord, I only want to do your will, show me your will." God always answers those who earnestly ask him with good intentions.

Is it all make-believe?

We can always be plagued by doubts. In dialoguing with Christ after Communion, is there not the possibility that we drift into a world of make-believe where it is not Christ that we communicate with, but where it is all going on in our own mind?

This is always a possibility, but we should note that God can speak to us in various ways: through the scriptures, using the words of our brothers and sisters. But above all he speaks to us using the means we have ourselves. God speaks to our reason using the tools of our reason, i.e. the mind. There are certain signs that can help in discerning whether we are listening to ourselves or to the voice of God:

• When it proposes courses of action that are not according to our tastes, or even the opposite of what we would be inclined to do.

• When it reminds us of our duties and prepares the way for us to accept the truth and incites us to do good.

• When it speaks words of good sense.

• When it brings us serenity and peace.

These are all good signs that can help us to discern God's voice.

One thing is certain. To really reflect on our lives and our duties, to scrutinize ourselves with absolute honesty before God, - will not all our efforts need the help of God himself? Surely God will not wash his hands of the effort that we make in his presence.

For this reason listening is a useful and good thing to do, and is perhaps the only way in which we can reflect on God's will. In fact, listening is a duty and the most natural response to Christ's visit.

How long should we spend listening to God?

This seems like a theoretical question that perhaps, there is no need even to ask. In fact, we would never ask ourselves such a question if a friend we were truly interested in came to visit.

It is unthinkable that, before the visit of a dear friend, we should estimate how long we will bother to spend with him. Nor would we plan how long to spend on the various parts of his visit. So many minutes of welcome, so many minutes to offer something to eat, twenty minutes listening etc... All that happens during the joyful visit of a friend is that we enjoy his company and he enjoys ours.

If we really feel it is necessary to ask how long we should spend listening to the Lord, then the answer is simple: as long as possible!

Since our meeting with Christ is a spiritual one we always run the risk of passing each other like ships in the night. Therefore it should not seem strange if we do organize our time at least a little, so we can profit of it better than if we had not done so. In fact our love for

Christ encourages us to make the most of the time we can spend with him.

Therefore we can legitimately ask: how long should we spend in listening? The answer lies in how long it takes to achieve a profound state of concentration.

This varies greatly from person to person. But normally in order to concentrate we need a time of peace and tranquility. A good start is to use the time immediately after Holy Communion to express our joy and gratitude to God, offering to Christ what seems best at that moment. Later, it would be good to give over at least fifteen minutes in the day to re-establishing contact with Jesus.

Ideally, we listen to Christ immediately after taking Communion but if this is not possible, it is not a problem. God exists outside time, so even later in the day we can pick up where we left off and complete our Communion.

For him, neither time nor space matter. He is always ready and willing to welcome us and ready to converse with us if we truly want.

If we take a quarter of an hour to relive our Holy Communion we will gain much from it.

Firstly it gives us the chance to choose the best time during the day when we can concentrate, and to choose the most suitable place. In a quarter of an hour we can usually reach a sufficient level of concentration.

This time of prayer and calm can also have a deep effect on our day. If we take a moment out of our chores and give some time to Christ, then the effect it can have on the subsequent duties of the day is enormous. It can calm our anxieties, make us reassess our problems and infuse all our actions with the strength of Christ.

What methods should we use to help us concentrate?

There are many ways and the best way is often dictated by each person's own experience. It is always useful to hear the experience of others in order to choose the best way for ourselves.

The most important thing is to put oneself in a state of interior calm. Choose a suitable position in which to calm your body. Certain bodily positions can also help our concentration while others can hinder it.

If you are lying on a sofa, you can't concentrate at all (or at least it's very difficult). If instead you choose a quiet place, you kneel down, close your eyes, and search for an inner silence, concentration becomes simple.

When you have created a calm and peaceful atmosphere, then you are ready to speak to Christ, but what do you say?

A word from the scriptures can help, such as "Speak Lord, your servant is listening". Alternatively you can ask the Lord what he wants from you. Another possibility is the statement of Thomas before the risen Christ: "My

Lord and my God". You could alternatively repeat Peter's words after hearing Jesus speak of the bread of life: "Lord, you alone have words of eternal life".

There is however a simpler prayer, the shortest of them all: "Jesus!" which means "Saviour!". Blessed are those who have learnt to pray using just one word: they will reach a deeper level of prayer.

In listening should we be active or passive?

It all depends on the manner in which one concentrates. There are those who can concentrate without the use of words. To be in the presence of Christ saying nothing is beautiful, but difficult. When our life is difficult or troubled, it seems impossible.

For those who find it more difficult, it is better to be active during this period of concentration. One simple way of doing this is to calmly repeat a short prayer.

However, the major difficulty lies in communicating with Christ. For this reason, once a suitable atmosphere has been created, it is advisable to follow the guidelines we have already looked at:

• Place before Christ the actions and duties we are about to undertake, asking him what his will is for us in our situation.

• Think about the people we will come into contact with after our meeting with Christ. We should ask him how he expects us to act and behave.

If this seems too much, it's enough to stay in silence before Christ or to repeat constantly a simple but meaningful prayer. Some people find Christ's prayer in the Garden of Gethsemane helpful: "Father, let your will be done, not mine".

What happens when I am constantly distracted in my thoughts?

Sometimes concentration is made so difficult by constant distractions, that those fifteen minutes of listening become a battle to overcome unprayerful thoughts. However, it is possible to use these distractions: the fire of prayer can be lit using the wood of distraction.

These disruptions tend to converge on what we consider important, such as our problems and worries. Why, then, should not we use this opportunity to put before God the problem we are worrying about? Why not bring this problem to Christ, asking Him: "Lord what do you want me to do about this problem? Show me what your will is!".

While you are praying about this problem, you may be distracted again. Don't lose heart; examine

this other distraction in turn: in the second distraction
you may find another important problem. Once again
use the opportunity to ask God to make his will clear
to you.

How difficult it is to stay 15 minutes with the Lord!

It is true: the most difficult task for us is to
concentrate. That is the reason why we do not do it
often.

It is much easier to do something else, rather than
think. To talk, read, or wonder is easier than to
concentrate our thought on ourselves, in order to really
ask what the will of God is. If we learn to concentrate,
we learn to think. If we make a habit of reflecting, we
learn to control ourselves. If we know how to control
ourselves, we know how to live.

A father of the desert says "Concentration is like the
wick of the candle." We cannot light a candle if the
wick is missing; and in the same way we cannot light
the candle of prayer without the wick of concentration.
Prayer is not possible without concentration, and our
Communion can be useless if we have not first reached
a sufficient level of concentration.

The real problem

It is important to be clear that the difficulty is not to be silent in order that God may speak to us. This is not our worry: it is his and his alone. The problem lies elsewhere. We must not put obstacles in God's path and make it difficult for him to speak to us.

God will choose when and how to speak to us, but we must do all that we can to facilitate his communication with us. It is in the period after Communion that God will ask us if we have done this. When he sees fit, God will speak to us and clarify the situation.

Often God speaks through his silence. Often God does not speak because he knows we are not ready to listen. There are also moments in which he speaks and we hear nothing at all.

CELEBRATING AND CONVERSING

After receiving Communion, our first sign of gratitude should be to celebrate Christ! Why? For seven reasons:

1. Simply for what is happening

Is it not obvious that we should be full of joy to see Christ coming to us? If we are not full of joy at meeting Him it is a sign that we have surely not understood what is happening. Can this personal meeting with Christ be unimportant?

As we go through the day so many shallow things bring us joy. How much more joy should we gain from Christ who comes exclusively and personally to meet us, and become one with us?

2. Good manners

When we meet a friend, seeing them brings us happiness. When we open the door to a relative we greet him with joy. Some people receive Communion as though they were going to a funeral; this cannot be what Christ wants. It is simply good manners therefore to be happy to receive him.

3. Joy awakens faith

In order to awaken faith we must begin with a reflection, an act of faith. If we feel real joy at meeting Christ it is a sign that we have received faith.

Faith is a gift that goes hand in hand with reflection. There is no room in faith for superficiality. The effort of expressing our joy to Christ opens us to him and therefore awakens our faith.

4. Joy is gratitude

This Joy should be our immediate and spontaneous answer to what we have received. It is an answer that lacks depth but it is the beginning of a more meaningful response. Our gratitude for this personal meeting will become deeper, but it begins at this moment. This is its first stage, and that is already worth something.

5. Joy initiates a conversation between friends

If we receive Christ with joy it allows our relationship with him to become a mature and truthful one. By gauging the way that people receive us, we understand how our relationship with them is progressing. If the reception is warm we put aside any judgments we may have had; but if the reception is cold we know exactly what to expect.

A warm welcome paves the way for a fruitful conversation. The way in which we welcome or don't welcome the other, can either put a seal on our friendship or damage it. In refusing to celebrate Christ we lessen our intimacy with him.

6. Celebrating Jesus is a good start

A cold reception of the Eucharist is certainly a bad start. Deciding whether or not to welcome Christ is the first stage, but it is not the most important stage - (we have already seen that listening is the most important part). However, if we do not welcome Christ it will surely affect our willingness to listen to him. Making the right decision at this juncture enables us to live the sacrament fully and receive everything that Christ has to give and tell us.

7. Welcoming Christ, the wellspring of joy

If we rejoice we are already in his intimate presence because Christ is joy, the joy of the Father and everyone's ultimate happiness. Welcoming him with joy means imitating him, being on the same wavelength as him. That joy already comes from him, for the world 'needs joy more than it needs bread'.

Communion with Christ is Communion with joy, and if we do this we raise the level of joy of the whole world.

We already begin to exercise charity and to bring hope, courage and enthusiasm to the world.

Isn't our celebration a little forced?

No, it is an act of faith. It is a rational and logical reaction, in fact it is a duty. But it is difficult for this attitude of celebration to come by itself, simply because our relationship with God goes beyond our five senses. It is a reflective act, not a natural or spontaneous one: we see nothing, we hear nothing.

It is an act of faith which has its roots in the depths of ourselves. It is an action which begins with our preparation but is mysteriously completed and brought to perfection by the Holy Spirit. As with every act of faith, it is rooted in our conviction, our reflection and in our love. It requires our good will and application.

Celebration is not an irrational emotion but a rational act. It is not a feeling that comes without encouragement, it is rather, an interior emotion which comes to the surface only if it expresses a deeply held joy.

How can we express our joy?

Each person must find the best way for themselves. The time of our great meeting with Christ is characterised by a solemn intimacy which is at the same time powerful and extremely personal. It is a powerful event that takes place in the silence of our hearts and minds. Therefore the joy that we express will often be equally invisible in its expression. We may well have no one to show it to, but there is no need to make it public.

We may find it useful to express our joy through deep gratitude, which does not require many words but which will find its expression in a deeply felt 'thank you' to Christ. This can sometimes be the best way of expressing our joy at his presence.

We can also extend our thank you over a longer period of time, long after we have left the church building. There is no need for complicated additions or elaborations; our conviction and happiness is enough. As we repeat our warmest thanks to Christ many feelings can enrich our expressions of gratitude and joy.

We can conclude that celebrating Christ's coming is faith. Celebrating Christ is love, the beginning of a great love which has already accepted Christ as a gift, and begins to prepare us for our gift to him. Celebration is right and fitting and opens us to the Eucharistic grace that God offers us.

Does Christ listen but not speak?

Our intimacy with Christ needs expression. The most natural way is through dialogue. A conversation between two friends always has the immediate effect of putting both at ease with each other. When we enter into dialogue we truly communicate.

We have given the utmost importance to listening to Christ. But we have also seen that there are great difficulties in listening, and that for those who are new to it, these difficulties can seem insurmountable. Dialogue is simpler, and can be used by all, and serves as good training for listening.

The main problem lies in how to listen to Christ in Holy Communion, since often Christ within us seems to listen but not to speak. This is the never-ending drama of prayer, and we need to make an effort to confront it.

We must confront the main objection which often surfaces: "Jesus fails to answer to what I say, so dialogue is impossible. I am simply engaged in a one-way conversation, or at best a two-way conversation with myself, where I provide both the questions and the answers".

Dialogue with God is not a game of make-believe, and neither is our conversation with Christ during Holy Communion. Here is the proof:

• The person of Christ exists and dwells within me in a mysterious but real way.

• The person of Christ within me listens in a mysterious but real way.

• The person of Christ within me stays silent but acts through his grace.

• The person of Christ within me loves, and therefore is always in dialogue with me, because dialogue consists of a love that is expressed.

But why does Christ not reveal himself to my senses? He is able to do so but normally does not, and nor should we expect him to. This is the way in which we communicate with God until we see him face to face (as St Paul explains). Even Christ, when he was with us on earth, accepted to communicate with the Father in this way. It is difficult to dialogue when only we seem to speak, but even Christ did that.

Let us not expect to hear anything with our ears

Guard yourself against those who often say: "God told me..." It is a dangerous phrase, because our communication with God always takes place under a veil of shadow and obscurity so that we can never say with absolute certainty "God said to me". At most we can say "It seems to me that I have received this inspiration" but more than that we cannot say.

After all, everything that God had to say to us has been written down in the scriptures. The gospel encompasses every situation and is very clear. But it can be very difficult to do always what the gospels literally require. So God also speaks to us veiled in mystery.

If we look at the dialogue between Jesus and His Father in the Garden of Gethsemane we see Christ in the depths of sadness, and he cries out to the Father "take this cup away from me". What is God's response? We can infer his response from Jesus' answer: "Father, let your will be done, not mine."

We should not expect a dialogue with God that we can perceive with our senses but we can expect some pointers. In fact Christ often speaks with a clarity that can take us by surprise.

It is a mysterious phenomenon that each and every person can experience that God speaks in impressive ways. We need only wait with good sense and balance and with a calm spirit. If we give him the time and space in which to answer, Christ will answer.

What shall we speak about with him? What interests you, interests Christ! With Christ within you, start to speak with him about your most serious problems, your pains and your joys. Persevere in this dialogue for it predisposes us to listen.

Christ naturally needs some silence in which to speak, and this is always what is missing from us. He needs great honesty from us and a thirst for the truth. Christ does not communicate with our masks. But he does speak to us and we must make every effort to experience this.

Let us not be afraid to feel too warm an affection for Christ; rather we should fear losing our feelings for him. We are not corpses unable to feel emotion; and Christ, much less so.

OFFERING AND ASKING

Jesus said to Simon: "You see this woman? I came into your house, and you poured no water over my feet, but she has poured out her tears over my feet and wiped them away with her hair. You gave me no kiss, but she has been covering my feet with kisses ever since I came in. You did not anoint my head with oil, but she has anointed my feet with ointment. For this reason I tell you that her sins, her many sins, must have been forgiven her, or she would not have shown such great love. It is the man who is forgiven little who shows little love." (*Luke* 7:44-47)

If a friend arrives, it is not enough to celebrate his arrival. We should hurry to offer him something, but what should we choose? Whatever would please our friend most, the best we have in the house, and if we have nothing in the house we should do our best to find something. At worst we could go out to buy something. But we would never do nothing at all.

When Christ comes to us, we should have something ready for him. But we need to judge what would please him best, and we need to ask ourselves what he would expect of us.

Jesus wants our lives to be in order in two areas in particular: in faithfulness to his commandments and in living according to his will, to what we see as his plan for our lives. It is precisely in these areas that we have to look for something that will please Christ. Search especially in the following three areas:

- Charity to others.

- Duties.

- Renouncing evil.

Under these three headings: charity, duties and renouncing evil we can find all the good actions of our lives. Look carefully at your life and search out those things that will please Christ in these three vital areas. Offer him what you find with enthusiasm. It is even better if we ask Christ to help us in our search.

Charity

Ask him what he expects most from us, what we have yet to give him and whether there are things that we should have done and have deliberately failed to see.

More concretely we can ask if there is something Jesus wants from us in regard to the way we treat our closest family members, in our work or study or in our circle of friends or colleagues. Is there some area of selfishness that blocks us from fully living Christian charity?

Is there anybody we need to forgive? Do we hold any grudges or resentments? Do we do enough for the poor or the sick? Is there somebody we know whom we neglect?

In our house or workplace there is someone we find difficult to love and accept, whom we consider a burden, and it is that very person we should think about.

Duties

We need to question ourselves by questioning Christ:

- In what have I pleased you?

- Which of my duties have I neglected most?

- Which of my neglected duties affects me or others most?

- What attitude characterises the fulfillment of my duties; do I do them grudgingly, angrily or lazily?

- Have I committed some grave injustice in the fulfillment of my duties? Have I made amends for that injustice?

Renouncing evil

Also in this, the area to search is vast. I need to dig deep and ask whether there is something within me that I am ashamed of before Christ: bad habits, compromises with evil, laziness, hypocrisy, sinful attitudes or actions.

Make specific promises

There is a wide range of actions to choose from. If I ask Jesus to help me in my search he will certainly give some pointers.

Having examined what will please Christ best I can offer it to him. I can formulate some precise promises and undertakings to fulfill during the course of the day, for love of Christ.

Naturally they should be undertakings that are clear and relevant. It is difficult to be faithful to a promise if we are not clear what it entails. They should also be promises that are realistic and feasible. We should not offer something that is so difficult that we will not know how to do it. We cannot cheat a true friend.

The person who gets used to communicating with Christ in this way, will soon see abundant fruits in every Communion. They will see their Christian life make great progress. If we learn to speak with Christ in this way we will no longer let him down.

"I seek you, not your gift!"

Let us end these reflections with a passage taken from the *Imitation of Christ*. The author gives these words to Jesus:

What do I require of you other than that you endeavour to resign yourself entirely to me?

Whatsoever you give besides yourself I regard not; for I seek not your gift but yourself. As it would not be enough for you if you had all things but me, so neither can it please me whatever you give, as long as you do not offer yourself. Offer yourself to me, and give your whole self for God, and your offering will be accepted.

Look, I offered my whole self to the father for you and have given my whole body and blood for your food, that I might be all yours, and you might always be mine. But if you remain in your selfishness and do not offer yourself freely to my will, your offering is not complete and nor will there be a complete union between us.

Therefore, if you desire to obtain liberty and grace, before you offer your works you must make a free oblation of yourself into the hands of God.

The reason why so few become illuminated and internally free is because they do not wholly renounce themselves.

"My sentence stands firm 'none of you can be my disciple unless he gives up all his possessions'" (*Lk* 14:33).

"If therefore, you desire to be my disciple, offer up yourself to me with all that you love" (*Imitation of Christ*, Bk 4 Ch 8).

Christ comes bearing gifts

At the end of our meeting with Christ it is also good to ask. It is not proper to do it immediately. It seems a little selfish to receive Communion and then immediately to ask... ask... ask.

Nevertheless Christ always comes bearing gifts and he gives them to us even when we do not ask. He gives us what we need most and does so with great generosity. There is always the danger, however, that we concentrate more on the gift than the giver, on his grace rather than his word. This is tantamount to religious consumerism, and does not help us at all.

After all this time dedicated to listening to Christ and entering into a dialogue with him, he expects that we ask him for something. The problem is what to ask for? Here we must be wise: the most important thing to ask for is his friendship, that we be faithful to him, because through this comes every other gift: "Seek first the kingdom of God, and all the rest will be given you as well."

A wise father does not do his children's homework

Ask to be faithful to Christ, this is the most vital thing. But do not ask to be faithful forever: it is neither wise nor according to Christ's teachings. In the model of prayer that he gave us (the 'Our Father'), Christ told us to ask for our daily bread i.e. what we need for today not for tomorrow. There is great wisdom in seeking only what we need day by day. It keeps us on our toes and always ready to do what Christ has in mind for us.

It is too simplistic for us to try to eliminate our problems once and for all. God wants us to play our part every day.

When a child says that he is not capable of doing his homework and asks for help, a wise father will not do the work for the child but help him to do it himself. He does this so that the child will not become lazy, but will learn something new.

God does the same thing when we ask. God is not some kind of automatic dispenser of answered prayers, and neither is prayer some kind of magic formula. God wants from us prayer which is intelligent and which helps us to become co-responsible with him for our lives, prayer which helps us to grow and mature.

When we pray we ask for what we need with faith, but God also awaits our contribution. Asking God to remain faithful to him for a day, for half a day or even for an hour is a judicious way for him to fill us with good will for that day or hour. If we are well disposed God can work within us.

God's time is not our time

Perhaps it is also important to explain another point: often God does not answer our prayers immediately. God is in the habit of turning up a fashionable quarter of an hour late. But always he does arrive, if we ask with faith humility and constancy. And when he does arrive he brings much more than the little we ask for.

God's timing is of great significance, and is ordered to our growth and maturation in faith, humility and love. When God's answer is late in coming it is already a great help, for it is in that period of waiting that we can begin to do our part.

The time we spend waiting for God is the time in which we grow, in which we reflect on our own responsibilities, open ourselves to faith and understand our powerlessness. Once we have seen that we can do nothing, our abandonment to God's will grows, and that time of waiting becomes the time in which we earn at least some of what God wants to give us.

When God does not answer our prayer

God always answers when we pray without ceasing. It is enough to try it to see that this is true.

And when God really doesn't answer our prayer, what is our response? If a child asks his father for the moon he will not be given it. When God does not give us what we ask for, it means that we too are asking for the moon, for something that we do not need, or something that would harm us. God always answers our prayer, and always gives more than we ask for.

You cannot believe it if you haven't experienced it. So why wait, experience it and believe!

Conclusion

We conclude with the words of Christ himself: "I am standing at the door knocking. If one of you hears me calling and opens the door, I will come in to share a meal at that person's side." (*Rev* 3:20)